The Rules of a Little Boss

A book of self-love

By

Haelee P. Moone

The Rules of a Big Boss LLC
Knightdale, NC 27545

This book is dedicated to:
Lael Swinton and Cameron Penix

I will not promise you that the road will be easy as you grow up. What I can promise you is that it will be fun and that I will do my best to be there for you each step of the way. My hope is that this book will serve as a roadmap to make things somewhat easier for you as you grow up. I hope that you find it helpful. And who knows, maybe we can write one together when you grow older. Good luck, Godspeed, and I love you.

Introduction

A lot of people struggle with who they are. These struggles are particularly prevalent in adolescents and young adults. Attempting to fit in can cause you to lose sight of who and what you truly are. I can say this as a matter of fact because it happened to me.

It takes courage to step out of your shell and be yourself. Being yourself is acceptance of your own unique beauty and knowing that no one else is like you. It takes time to get to this point so you won't get there overnight. Please know that there are no shortcuts and that you can't rush it. You will pick up key ingredients along the way so take your time and enjoy the journey. I promise that it will be delicious in the end.

While I can help inspire you, I can't make you more confident in yourself. You must be willing to do the work expressed within this book to achieve higher self-esteem. The things contained within are what helped me when I was your age. My hope is that these things help you as they did me. Good luck, Godspeed, I hope you enjoy it, and thank you for your purchase!

Being yourself is acceptance of your own value and beauty.

You are naturally gorgeous because you are kissed by the sun's brightest rays.

Always be yourself no matter what and don't apologize for it.

Experiment on yourself so you can find your own inner beauty.

Wear what makes you happy [appropriately of course] and be proud of it!

You shine everywhere you go.

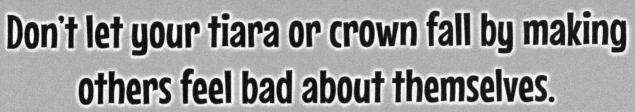

Don't let your tiara or crown fall by making others feel bad about themselves.

Use haters as motivation and step around them.

Don't let people pressure you into doing anything you know is wrong.

When you try to change yourself to please all these people you will be unhappy and push away those who genuinely love you

Treat yourself and others with kindness and respect.

Vibe sessions are where you turn the music on, put together a outfit, and just allow yourself to feel your best.

Love and appreciate yourself because you're stuck with yourself.

Don't let anyone bully you or make you feel bad about yourself.

You have the strength of a superhero. You can get through anything.

THE END

Acknowledgments

I have been through some dark times in my young life. I guess it was all for a purpose however in that they helped me write this book. That lets me know that my pain had a purpose. It lets me know that my life has purpose. On that note, I would like to take a moment to thank and acknowledge the following people in helping me put this entire thing together.

I would like to thank God for his grace and mercies that renew daily.

I would like to thank my Grandparents Wanda R. Moone, Terrence G. Westry, and Gilbert E. Baltimore for their old sayings, wisdom, and support.

I would like to honor and thank my Dad, Dedrick L. Moone for supporting and being there for me no matter what.

I would like to honor my mom for providing emotional support and teaching me affirmations.

I would like to thank Dr. Vanessa J. Raynor for help, being patient with me, and being a mentor.

I would like to thank Myanna and Rachel for being my closest friends outside of myself (LOL).

I would like to thank my dog, Oreo for providing emotional support.

I unfortunately do not have enough space to acknowledge everyone. But do know that you are appreciated and loved.

Contact the Author

You can connect or contact me via social media or the web. Details are provided below. I hope to hear from you.

 https://www.thebookofselflove.com/

 @thebookofselflove2020

 @thebookofselflove2020

 @The Rules of a Big boss

Also by Haelee Moone

The Rules of a Big Boss: A book of self-love

The Unexpected Journey: Fire and Gold.

Don't Miss Out!

Go to the link below and you can sign up to receive emails whenever Haelee Moone publishes a new book. There is no obligation or commitment.

https://books2read.com/author/x/subscribe/1/261406/?preferred_retailer=0&book=726635

CPSIA information can be obtained
at www.ICGtesting.com
Printed in the USA
LVHW072232261221
706816LV00026B/420